D0852570

MAY   2015

SETTING
THE STAGE
FOR FLUENCY

My Sprig of Lilac

Remembering Abraham Lincoln

by Wim Coleman and Pat Perrin
illustrated by Dominic Catalano

RED
CHAIR
·PRESS·

Please visit our website at **www.redchairpress.com** for more high-quality products for young readers.

 EDUCATORS: Find FREE lesson plans and a Readers' Theater script for this book at www.redchairpress.com/free-activities.

About the Authors

Wim Coleman and **Pat Perrin** are a husband and wife who write together. Their more-than-100 publications include plays, stories, articles, essays, books, classroom materials, and mainstream fiction. Wim has a BFA in Theatre Arts and an MAT in English and Education from Drake University. Pat has a BA in English from Duke, an MA in Liberal Studies from Hollins University, and a PhD in Art Theory and Criticism from the University of Georgia. Both have classroom teaching experience. For 13 years they lived in the beautiful Mexican town of San Miguel de Allende, where they created and managed a scholarship program for at-risk students under the auspices of San Miguel PEN. Some of their stories draw on Mexican myth and tradition. Their highly-praised works for young readers include award-winning historical fiction, popular collections of plays, and a "nonfiction" book about unicorns.

My Sprig of Lilac: Remembering Abraham Lincoln

Publisher's Cataloging-In-Publication Data
(Prepared by The Donohue Group, Inc.)

Coleman, Wim.
My sprig of lilac : remembering Abraham Lincoln / by Wim Coleman and Pat Perrin ; illustrated by Dominic Catalano.

p. : ill. ; cm. -- (Setting the stage for fluency)

Summary: Abraham Lincoln, the 16th President of the United States, preserved the union of the nation, but after the Civil War he struggled with Congress and the people over Reconstruction. Despite the war and political strife, Lincoln's life and legacy touched the hearts of millions. This play draws upon the writings of many of those people and from Lincoln himself. Includes special book features for further study and a special section for teachers and librarians.
Interest age level: 009-012.
Includes bibliographical references.
ISBN: 978-1-939656-54-4 (lib. binding/hardcover)
ISBN: 978-1-939656-59-9 (pbk.)
ISBN: 978-1-939656-55-1 (eBk)

1. Lincoln, Abraham, 1809-1865--Juvenile drama. 2. Presidents--United States--Biography--Juvenile drama. 3. United States--Politics and government--1865-1869--Juvenile drama. 4. Lincoln, Abraham, 1809-1865--Drama. 5. Presidents--United States--Biography--Drama. 6. United States--Politics and government--1865-1869--Drama. 7. Children's plays, American. 8. Historical drama. 9. Biographical drama. I. Lincoln, Abraham, 1809-1865. Works. Selections. II. Perrin, Pat. III. Catalano, Dominic. IV. Title.

PS3553.O47448 My 2014
[Fic]   2013956255

Photo page 39: Shutterstock

This series first published by:
Red Chair Press LLC   PO Box 333   South Egremont, MA 01258-0333

Printed in the United States of America

1 2 3 4 5 18 17 16 15 14

TABLE OF CONTENTS

INTRODUCTION

Abraham Lincoln was the 16th President of the United States. He was President from March 1861 until April 1865. The Civil War began soon after he took office.

In 1863, Lincoln issued an official announcement called the Emancipation Proclamation. (*Emancipation* means being freed from something.) The proclamation freed many slaves and also protected escaped slaves.

On April 14, 1865, an assassin shot and killed President Lincoln. This play takes place at Lincoln's funeral. The setting is the East Room of the White House. The president's body lies "in state." That means that the casket is placed where people can come to see it and pay their respects. The casket was open for a last view of the honored president.

After lying in state at the White House, Abraham Lincoln's body was put on a train. For three weeks, the *Lincoln Special* traveled slowly to Springfield, Illinois. All along the way people gathered at the tracks to honor the president.

Most of the characters in this play are real people who could have been at the funeral. Three of the characters are the ghosts of people who knew Lincoln when they were alive.

Most of the scenes take place at the funeral. Some of the story takes place in a character's memories. Abraham Lincoln appears only in those memories.

THE CAST OF CHARACTERS

Narrators 1, 2, and 3

Living characters:

Mourners 1, 2, 3, and 4

Mary Todd Lincoln, Abraham Lincoln's widow

Edwin M. Stanton, Secretary of War to Abraham Lincoln

Frederick Douglass, ex-slave and abolitionist

Sojourner Truth, ex-slave and famous speechmaker

Horace Greeley, newspaper editor

Walt Whitman, poet

In memory:

Abraham Lincoln

Ghosts:

Willie Lincoln, Lincoln's son, died 1862

Stephen A. Douglas, Lincoln's political rival, died 1861

John Wilkes Booth, Lincoln's assassin, died 1865

Future voices:

Rosa Parks

Martin Luther King Jr.

Setting: the East Room of the White House.
Time: April 18, 1865, plus some past
and future events

SCENE ONE

Narrator 1: This is a time of mourning. All-too-familiar words are spoken …

Narrator 2: … well-meaning words, but too much used …

Narrator 3: … even at the funeral of a great man.

Mourner 1: I share your sorrow.

Mourner 2: My deepest sympathies.

Mourner 3: I'm sorry for your loss.

Mourner 4: The nation grieves with you.

Narrator 1: Mary Todd Lincoln takes little comfort in such talk.

Mary Todd Lincoln: Thank you … You are most kind … I'm glad you're here …

Narrator 2: It is April 18, 1865, at the White House …

Narrator 3: President Abraham Lincoln's body lies in state in the East Room.

Narrator 1: Just four days ago, the president was killed.

Narrator 2: He was murdered by an **assassin**.

Narrator 3: He was shot during a play at Ford's Theatre in Washington, D.C.

Narrator 1: Now this huge room is decorated in black.

Narrator 2: There are also many flowers.

Narrator 3: Some 25 thousand people line up to pay their respects.

Narrator 1: Just five days before the president's death, the Civil War ended. The Confederate Army surrendered. The Union was saved. It was Lincoln's greatest moment of triumph.

Narrator 2: A man steps toward Mrs. Lincoln. He takes her by the hand. It is Lincoln's Secretary of War, Edwin Stanton.

Edwin M. Stanton: Now he belongs to the ages.[1]

Mary Todd Lincoln: At last, someone has said something worth saying.

Narrator 3: A powerfully-built but noble-looking man approaches the widow. He once was a slave. Now he is a famous **abolitionist**.

Edwin M. Stanton: Mrs. Lincoln, I believe you know Frederick Douglass.

Mary Todd Lincoln: My husband admired your honesty and brilliance. He said you kept him up to the mark.

Frederick Douglass: I'm humbled, Mrs. Lincoln.

Narrator 1: An African-American woman in her sixties steps toward the widow.

Frederick Douglass: Allow me to introduce Sojourner Truth. She is another former slave.

Mary Todd Lincoln: My husband called you a woman of great courage.

Sojourner Truth: Thank you, Mrs. Lincoln.

Mary Todd Lincoln: He was stirred by both of your stories. You escaped from slavery to freedom. Then you rose up to be leaders. Both of you have inspired mistreated people everywhere.

Narrator 2: A short, narrow-shouldered gentleman also comes forward.

Edwin M. Stanton: And I'm sure you've met Horace Greeley. He is the editor of the *New York Tribune*.

Mary Todd Lincoln: My husband enjoyed his lively arguments with you, Mr. Greeley.

Horace Greeley: The pleasure was mine, Mrs. Lincoln.

Narrator 3: Mrs. Lincoln draws the war secretary, the newspaperman, and the two former slaves closer. She gathers the four visitors around her.

Mary Todd Lincoln: Stay near me, the four of you. You're the only souls who haven't tried to comfort me with empty words. You have a gift for saying little when there's too much to say.

Narrator 1: And of course, a funeral is a time to brood over lost chances …

Mary Todd Lincoln: He expected this to happen. He said so.

Edwin M. Stanton: How could he have known?

Mary Todd Lincoln: He knew things. One morning—oh, about two weeks ago …

(Memory begins)

Abraham Lincoln: Such a dream I've had, Mary.

Mary Todd Lincoln: *(remembering)* Such a dream, indeed!

Abraham Lincoln: There seemed to be a deathlike stillness about me. Then I heard soft sobs. It sounded like a number of people weeping. I thought I left my bed and wandered downstairs. Then the silence was broken by the same pitiful sobbing. But the mourners were invisible. I went from room to room. No living person was in sight. I saw light in all the rooms. But where were all the people who sounded as if their hearts would break? I was puzzled and alarmed. I kept on until I entered the East Room …

Mary Todd Lincoln: *(remembering)* This very room!

Abraham Lincoln: Before me was a corpse lying in state. I couldn't see its face. Around it were stationed soldiers who acted as guards. A crowd of people gazed upon the corpse, weeping pitifully. "Who is dead in the White House?" I asked one of the soldiers. "The President," he told me. "He was killed by an assassin." Then I woke from my dream. Only a dream—but it annoys me strangely, Mary.[2]

(Memory ends)

Mary Todd Lincoln: If only I'd paid better heed. He brooded quietly from that day on. But he never asked for better protection. And now—oh, unluckiest of days!

SCENE THREE

Narrator 2: A middle-aged, long-bearded man steps toward her.

Walt Whitman: Not so, ma'am, and be comforted.
Have you supposed it lucky to be born?
I hasten to inform you it is just as lucky to die, and I know it.[3]

Mary Todd Lincoln: How dare you, sir!

Edwin M. Stanton: Such words to a mourning widow! And why have you come in that shabby outfit? And take off that awful hat at once!

Walt Whitman: I wear my hat as I please indoors or out.

Edwin M. Stanton: Who are you?

Walt Whitman: Walt Whitman, at your service.

Horace Greeley: Oh, yes, the poet. Wrote a book of verses some years back—*Leaves of Grass.*

Edwin M. Stanton: What's a poor wandering poet doing at the funeral of a great man?

Walt Whitman: We were dearest of friends. Brothers, really.

Edwin M. Stanton: Really!

Mary Todd Lincoln: First I've heard of it!

13

Walt Whitman: I saw him almost every morning for a time. He'd be riding his horse on Vermont Street, near L Street. He was always surrounded by cavalry guards. But he and I exchanged friendly bows.[4]

Edwin M. Stanton: An exchange of bows from a distance. He didn't even know your name. Well. *That* certainly put you on warm terms with the late president.

Walt Whitman: It did. I knew him and loved him on behalf of all.

Mary Todd Lincoln: You are quite the most awful man.

Narrator 3: An 11-year-old boy approaches the president's widow.

Willie Lincoln: Listen to him. He is no more a fool than Papa. And he is as much a fool as Papa.

Edwin M. Stanton: What a strange thing to say, boy!

Mary Todd Lincoln: Willie, my dear son! You've returned to me!

Horace Greeley: Poor woman—she's gone mad. Willie died three years ago of **typhoid fever**.

Edwin M. Stanton: Mrs. Lincoln, please calm yourself. Your **grief** is playing tricks on you. *(to Willie)* And you— where are your parents?

Willie Lincoln: Look closer, Mr. Stanton. You know me.

Edwin M. Stanton: It *is* you! I met you when I first came to the White House—just before …

Willie Lincoln: Before I died.

Edwin M. Stanton: But how can this be?

Mary Todd Lincoln: Never mind how! I've got my lovely child back! Is anything *not* possible? And my husband— now—surely—!

Willie Lincoln: No, Mama.

Mary Todd Lincoln: But why? If you're here, why can't he come back?

Willie Lincoln: I'm only a boy. How can I know?

Horace Greeley: Am I dreaming this?

Walt Whitman: We must expect strange company on such a day.

Narrator 3: A short, broad-chested man steps toward the coffin.

Stephen A. Douglas: And so you've joined the dead, Mr. Lincoln. You sent more than 600,000 men to their deaths. Was it worth it? You've left the nation in a fine state of ruin.

Edwin M. Stanton: Do not speak ill of the dead, sir.

Stephen A. Douglas: Pardon me—but surely being dead myself gives me some right.

Mary Todd Lincoln: Why, Stephen Douglas!

Edwin M. Stanton: The "Little Giant"—dead nearly four years now. Do you think you could have done better for the nation, Senator?

Stephen A. Douglas: Could I have done much worse? I saw from the start where he would lead us. He had those fool notions about the Declaration of Independence. "All men are created equal!" He claimed that those words of 1776 meant to include black men as well as white.

Frederick Douglass: Could they have meant otherwise?

Stephen A. Douglas: Thomas Jefferson wrote the Declaration of Independence. Jefferson was the owner of a large number of slaves. He treated them as property. Did he intend to say that his Negro slaves were created as his equals? Did he mean that he was violating the law of God by holding them as slaves?[5]

Frederick Douglass: I think it possible that he meant just that.

Stephen A. Douglas: Well, Mr. Lincoln himself didn't believe that the races were equal. He said so himself …

(Memory begins)

Abraham Lincoln: I am not in favor of bringing about the social and political equality of the white and black races. I never have been.[6]

(Memory ends)

Stephen A. Douglas: So all men are created equal— except that they aren't.

SCENE SIX

Stephen A. Douglas: And what do you say, Mr. Douglass, former slave? What was your abolitionist's view of him?

Frederick Douglass: Not entirely happy—at least at first. He was most of all the white man's President. He was devoted to the welfare of white men.[7] And he was tardy in the cause of emancipation.

Horace Greeley: Yes, and let's not forget what cause he put first during the war. He made that clear enough in a letter to my newspaper …

(Memory begins)

Abraham Lincoln: I would save the Union. My main goal in this struggle is to save the Union. It is not to save or to destroy slavery. What I do about slavery, I do because it helps to save the Union.[8]

(Memory ends)

Edwin M. Stanton: And yet his Emancipation Proclamation lay in his desk drawer. It was already there when he wrote those words about the Union.

Frederick Douglass: That Proclamation left no question. American slavery was doomed. And it called upon men of color to fight for their freedom. Two hundred thousand of our people responded to the call. They went with muskets on their shoulders, and eagles on their buttons. They marched for liberty and union. They supported the national flag.[9] My own son among them.

SCENE SEVEN

Sojourner Truth: You say that President Lincoln didn't believe in equality? Looked down on men and women of my race? I'll not believe it. I got to meet him—October of last year, it was. He rose from his desk and bowed to me— oh, so courteous.[10]

(Memory begins)

Sojourner Truth: Mr. President, when you first ran for this office, I'd never heard of you.

Abraham Lincoln: I'd heard of *you* many times before that.

Sojourner Truth: When you got to be president, I worried sick over you. I thought you'd be torn to pieces by all that was going on.

Abraham Lincoln: That may yet be my fate.

Sojourner Truth: No, I'm sure it won't. You're the best president we've had.

Abraham Lincoln: I'm sure that's not true. I've done nothing that many who came before me wouldn't have done. George Washington himself, I expect.

Sojourner Truth: Why didn't they set slaves free?

Abraham Lincoln: Events didn't allow it. I do not claim to have controlled events. I confess that events have controlled me.[11] My fellow contrymen down south behaved badly. Finally I had no choice but to free their slaves. It wasn't up to me. And I didn't free all the slaves everywhere. There's more work to be done to make that happen. Your grandson is serving in the Union Army, isn't he?

Sojourner Truth: In the 54th Massachusetts Volunteer Infantry Regiment.

Abraham Lincoln: May he return safely to your arms.

Sojourner Truth: May they all return safe—all the men of both North and South.

Abraham Lincoln: Well wished. And well prayed.

(End of memory)

Sojourner Truth: I looked him straight in the eye that day. I didn't see an ounce of **prejudice** against me—not for being colored, not for being a woman.

Frederick Douglass: I know just what you mean. I didn't trust him at first. But then he turned to me for advice …[12]

(Memory begins)

Abraham Lincoln: Tell Governor Buckingham to wait a while. I want to have a long talk with my friend Frederick Douglass.

Frederick Douglass: *(remembering)* We discussed weighty matters.

Abraham Lincoln: The slaves are not joining the Union army as fast as I had hoped. Not enough of them are joining up.

Frederick Douglass: Slaveholders are crafty men. They know how to keep such things from their slaves. Probably very few of them even know of your proclamation.

Abraham Lincoln: Well, I want you to let them know about it. I hate slavery as much as you do. I want to see it ended completely. [13]

(Memory ends)

Frederick Douglass: *(remembering)* Certainly he had some prejudices. They were part of him. He as much as said so himself. And yet he never showed the slightest trace of it toward me.

Stephen A. Douglas: How do we explain such a contradictory man?

Narrator 1: A young, black-haired, handsome man approaches the coffin. He leans over and murmurs to the slain president …

John Wilkes Booth: *Sic semper tyrannis*—Thus always to **tyrants**!

Mary Todd Lincoln: That voice—those words!

John Wilkes Booth: I have done it! The South is avenged![14]

Mary Todd Lincoln: Shouted by the murderer as he made his escape!

Edwin M. Stanton: It's him—John Wilkes Booth! Guards! Seize this man!

Willie Lincoln: No need. He's only here in spirit.

Sojourner Truth: Another ghost?

Willie Lincoln: He might as well be. He'll be killed in the next few days. Shot to death in a burning barn.

John Wilkes Booth: Like some mad dog, then? Is that to be my fate? And for what? For slaying the worst tyrant ever known to all the world.

Mary Todd Lincoln: Will someone make him leave? He'll drive me mad.

Willie Lincoln: Let him stay, Mother.

Mary Todd Lincoln: What on earth for?

Willie Lincoln: We must try to understand why he did what he did.

Sojourner Truth: Hasn't that boy grown a bit? Isn't he a couple of inches taller than when we first caught sight of him?

Edwin M. Stanton: And his voice—isn't it deeper?

John Wilkes Booth: I had plots and plans to stop him. Plots and plans I laid to kidnap and stop him. All of them were in vain. Just a few days ago, he spoke from a White House window. I stood in a crowd listening to him …

(Memory begins)

Abraham Lincoln: We meet this evening, not in sorrow, but in gladness of heart. Our recent victories give us hope of a righteous and speedy peace.[15]

John Wilkes Booth: *(remembering)* Bragging, the tyrant was! Crowing over a victory that the South will never allow! But then— oh, worse and worse. He spoke of new amendments to the United States Constitution. Worse amendments than his evil Thirteenth. He had already ended African slavery. And slavery was one of the greatest blessings that God ever bestowed upon a favored nation.[16] Now negroes would parade in our midst as full citizens. They would vote and hold office. What was to stop them from ruling over whites?

Abraham Lincoln: It may soon be my duty to make some new announcement to the people of the South.

John Wilkes Booth: *(remembering)* No, never! I swore then and there, it was the last speech he would ever give.

(End of memory)

Edwin M. Stanton: And so you killed him for setting men free.

John Wilkes Booth: Fool. I killed him lest he make men of your noble color and mine into slaves. And someday, his name will be rightly condemned by everyone. Mine shall be spoken with honor.

Frederick Douglass: Be glad that you aren't here in body. In my slave days, I beat an **overseer** to within an inch of his life. But he gave me less cause than you do.

Willie Lincoln: He would not call you his enemy, Mr. Booth—not even now.

Edwin M. Stanton: Indeed, it was not a word he liked. I seldom heard him use it. Imagine—he was waging the most terrible war yet known to humankind. But he spoke seldom of enemies, always of friends …

(Memory begins)

Abraham Lincoln: We are not enemies, but friends. We must not be enemies. Strong feelings may have strained our love for one another. But rage must not break our bonds. We will once again become a Union. Then we will surely be guided by the better angels of our nature.[17]

(Memory ends)

SCENE TEN

Mary Todd Lincoln: All these ghosts—so why is my husband not among them?

Willie Lincoln: Oh, more than his ghost is here. He is part of every one of us. He is part of our democracy. My father believed that American democracy was greater than himself. He considered democracy greater than the limits of his own mind …

Abraham Lincoln: … constantly looked to, constantly labored for. Never perfectly accomplished. But democracy is constantly spreading. It is having its effect. It is making life more valuable for all people, of all colors, everywhere.

Willie Lincoln: I glimpse more and more of the future. Mr. Douglass, you'll serve as a champion to the downtrodden. Not just men of your own color. You'll fight for women's rights …

Frederick Douglass: *(In the future)* What right have I, what right have you, to deny to woman full and complete citizenship? What right has anybody who believes in government of the people, by the people, and for the people?[18]

Willie Lincoln: … but women won't be allowed to vote until long after you're in your grave. And even then, the struggle for sexual equality will barely have begun. Miss Truth, you'll board streetcars in Washington trying to desegregate them …

Sojourner Truth: *(In the future)* I have been forty years a slave and forty years free. I would be here forty years more to have equal rights for all.[19]

Willie Lincoln: … but it won't be until in 1955 that a woman named Rosa Parks will do likewise. She will strike a stunning blow for justice.

Rosa Parks: People always say that I didn't give up my seat because I was tired. That isn't true. No, the only tired I was, was tired of giving in.[20]

Willie Lincoln: In 1963, a descendant of slaves named Martin Luther King Jr. will be heard. He will stand before a great statue of my father. He will speak to a quarter of a million people. He will demand an end to centuries of racial injustice …

Martin Luther King Jr.: I have a dream that one day this nation will rise up and live out the true meaning of its own words. "We hold these truths to be self-evident that all men are created equal."

Willie Lincoln: Laws will be passed. Progress will be made. But this great-hearted leader will be slain like my father. He will be slain for fighting with no other weapon than his love for humankind.

Martin Luther King Jr.: No, no—we are not satisfied. We will not be satisfied until justice rolls down like waters and righteousness like a mighty stream.[21]

Willie Lincoln: I see no end to the struggle, none. For how can our nation's promise of justice and freedom ever be fulfilled for all? But don't be discouraged. Be brave. The struggle itself is what matters. Every mind is small. Every mind must grow. All minds must grow together.

Edwin M. Stanton: Soon the president must be carried away from here.

Mary Todd: No.

Edwin M. Stanton: You know what's to be done, Mrs. Lincoln. You agreed to it. The coffin will be taken by train to Springfield. Mourners will greet it along the way. It will pass through town after town after town for 13 days.

Mary Todd Lincoln: Who can imagine such a journey?

Willie Lincoln: The poet can. Hear him.

Narrator 2: The poet takes a blossom from his jacket. He places it on the corpse.

Walt Whitman:

> Coffin that passes through lanes and streets,
> Through day and night, with the great cloud darkening
> the land …
> With the waiting depot … and the sombre faces,
> With **dirges** through the night, with the thousand
> voices rising strong and solemn;
> With all the mournful voices of the dirges, pour'd
> around the coffin,
> The dim-lit churches and the shuddering organs—
> Where amid these you journey,
> With the tolling, tolling bells' perpetual clang;
> Here! coffin that slowly passes,
> I give you my sprig of lilac.[22]

WORDS TO KNOW

abolitionist: a person who favors getting rid of slavery

assassin: a person who murders someone for political or religious reasons

dirge: a funeral tune, or song in memory of the dead

grief: deep sorrow

overseer: man in charge of the slaves

prejudice: an opinion against something but not based on reason

typhoid fever: an infection that was deadly at the time of the play

tyrant: a cruel ruler

Read More

Books:
Freedman, Russell. *Abraham Lincoln & Frederick Douglass: The Story Behind an American Friendship.* Clarion Books, 2012.

Levin, Jonathan. *Poetry for Young People: Walt Whitman.* Sterling, 2008.

Stone, Tanya Lee. *Abraham Lincoln: A Photographic Story of a Life.* Dorling Kindersley, 2005.

SOURCE NOTES

Please Note: The quotes in this play are paraphrased from or adapted from the sources listed below.

[1] Words spoken by Stanton at Lincoln's deathbed

[2] Ward Hill Lamon, Recollections of Abraham Lincoln, *1847–1885*, 1911
(http://www.dreamtree.com/inside/?page_id=47) (According to Lamon, Lincoln told this to a group of people that included Mary Todd Lincoln.)

[3] two lines from Walt Whitman, "Song of Myself" (http://www.princeton.edu/~batke/logr/log_026.html)

[4] Walt Whitman, *Specimen Days*, August 12th, 1863
(http://www.bartleby.com/229/1045.html) (loosely paraphrased)

[5] Lincoln-Douglas debates of 1858 (http://www.claremontmckenna.edu/govt/jpitney/lincdoug.html)

[6] Lincoln-Douglas debates of 1858
(http://www.learner.org/workshops/primarysources/emancipation/docs/fourthdebate.html)

[7] Frederick Douglass, Oration in Memory of Abraham Lincoln, April 14, 1876; Delivered at the Unveiling of The Freedmen's Monument in Memory of Abraham Lincoln, Lincoln Park, Washington, D.C.
(http://teachingamericanhistory.org/library/index.asp?documentprint=39) (Douglass said "preeminently" instead of "most of all")

[8] Abraham Lincoln, letter to Horace Greeley for the *New York Tribune*, August 22, 1862
(http://en.wikipedia.org/wiki/Abraham_Lincoln_on_slavery)

[9] Frederick Douglass, Oration in Memory of Abraham Lincoln, op. cit.
(http://teachingamericanhistory.org/library/index.asp?documentprint=39)

[10] This scene is based on Sojourner Truth's own account of her meeting with Lincoln in a letter dictated by her to Rowland Johnson, reprinted in the 1875 edition of *The Narrative of Sojourner Truth: A Northern Slave*. (http://www.sojournertruth.org/Library/Speeches/Default.htm#LINCOLN) Truth didn't mention discussing her son having joined the Union Army, however added to play to make important point.

[11] This is from Lincoln's letter to Albert G. Hodges, April 4, 1864; he is referring to his motives in issuing the Emancipation Proclamation. (http://showcase.netins.net/web/creative/lincoln/speeches/hodges.htm)

[12] The following conversation follows closely Douglass's account in *Life and Times of Frederick Douglass: His Early Life as a Slave, His Escape from Bondage, and His Complete History to the Present Time* (http://www.mrlincolnswhitehouse.org/inside.asp?ID=38&subjectID=2)

[13] Although Douglass didn't include this sentence in his account of the meeting, it is considered likely that Lincoln said it then. (http://www.mrlincolnswhitehouse.org/inside.asp?ID=38&subjectID=2)

[14] Booth shouted *"Sic semper tyrannis"* when he leapt to the stage after shooting Lincoln. According to some reports, he added, "I have done it, the South is avenged!"

[15] This and the following Lincoln quote are from his last public address, April 11, 1865; Booth heard it and vowed to kill Lincoln because of it.
(http://quod.lib.umich.edu/cgi/t/text/text-idx?q1=suffrage;rgn=div1;c=lincoln;view=text;type=simple;cc=lincoln;subview=detail;sort=occur;idno=lincoln8;node=lincoln8%3A850)

[16] Booth described slavery thus in a sealed letter opened after his death.
(http://en.wikipedia.org/wiki/John_Wilkes_Booth#cite_note-NYTltr-141)

[17] Abraham Lincoln, First Inaugural Address, March 4, 1861
(http://en.wikisource.org/wiki/Abraham_Lincoln%27s_First_Inaugural_Address)

[18] Frederick Douglass, speech at the Woman Suffrage meeting in Tremont Temple, Boston, May 24, 1886
(http://teachingamericanhistory.org/library/index.asp?document=494)

[19] Sojourner Truth, address to the first annual meeting of the American Equal Rights Association, May 9, 1867

[20] Parks, Rosa; James Haskins (1992). *Rosa Parks: My Story*.
(http://en.wikipedia.org/wiki/Rosa_parks#cite_note-autobiography1-20)

[21] Two quotes from Martin Luther King Jr.'s I Have a Dream Speech, August 28, 1963 Washington, DC.

[22] Walt Whitman, "When Lilacs Last in the Dooryard Bloom'd"
(http://en.wikisource.org/wiki/Leaves_of_Grass/Book_XXII#When_Lilacs_Last_in_the_Dooryard_Bloom.27d)